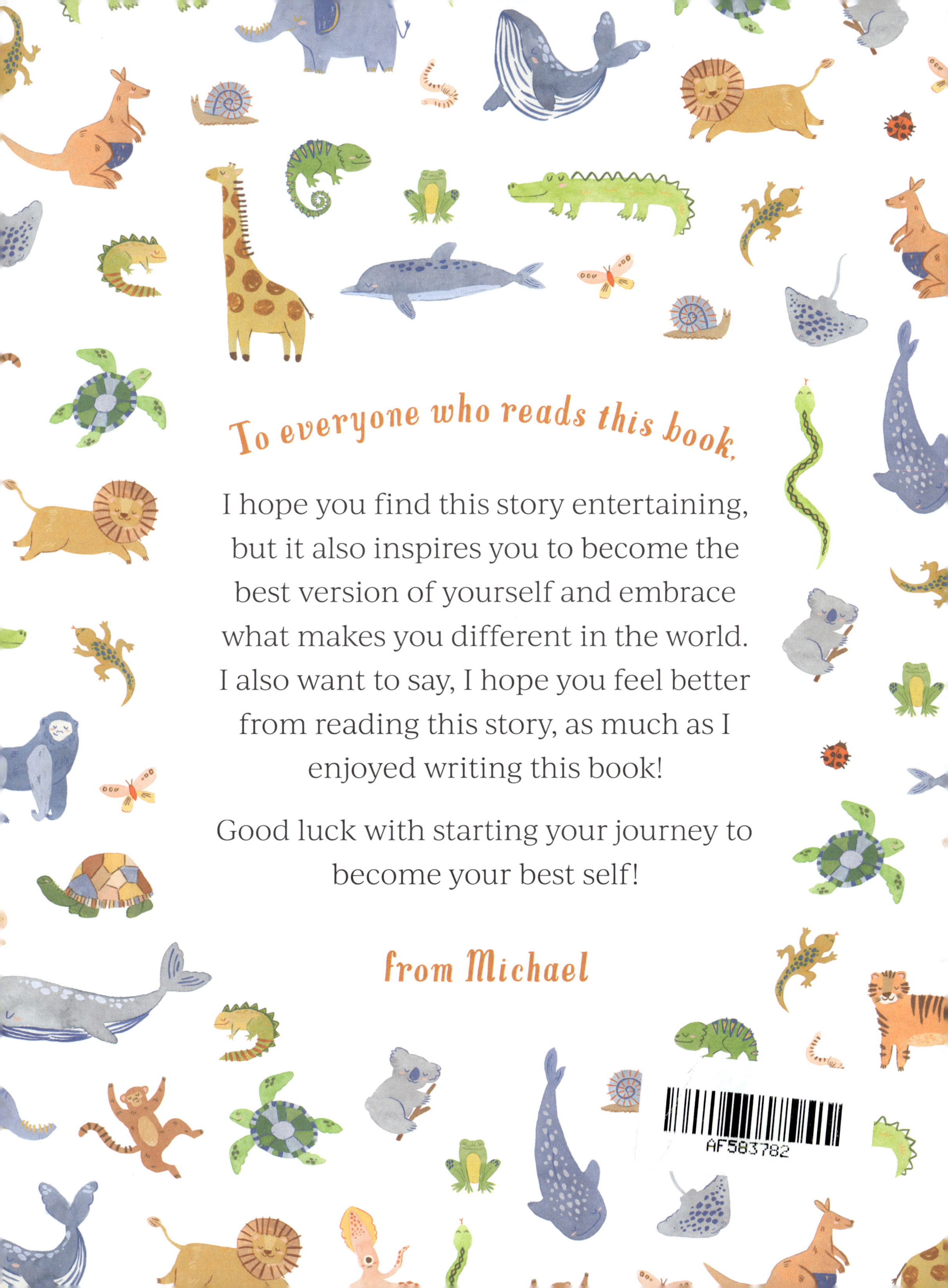

To everyone who reads this book,

I hope you find this story entertaining, but it also inspires you to become the best version of yourself and embrace what makes you different in the world. I also want to say, I hope you feel better from reading this story, as much as I enjoyed writing this book!

Good luck with starting your journey to become your best self!

from Michael

Scholastic Press

An imprint of Scholastic Australia Pty Limited (ABN 11 000 614 577)
PO Box 579 Gosford NSW 2250
www.scholastic.com.au

Part of the Scholastic Group
Sydney • Auckland • New York • Toronto • London • Mexico City • New Delhi • Hong Kong • Buenos Aires • Puerto Rico

Published by Scholastic Australia in 2026.

Photograph of Michael Theo by Andres Marin.

A catalogue record for this book is available from the National Library of Australia

ISBN: 978-1-76172-094-9
Typeset in Ivy Journal.
The illustrations in this book were made with watercolour, gouache, and coloured pencil with some digital final touches.

Book design by Astred Hicks.

We acknowledge the Traditional Owners of the Country on which we live and work.
We pay respect to Elders past and present.

Printed in China by RR Donnelley.
Scholastic Australia's policy, in association with RR Donnelley, is to use papers that are renewable and made efficiently with wood from responsibly managed sources, so as to minimise its environmental footprint.
10 9 8 7 6 5 4 3 2 1 26 27 28 29 30 / 2

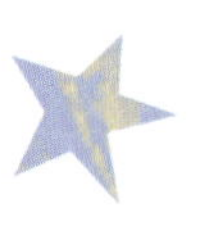

Edward's Astonishing Animals

Michael Theo Ella Brissenden

A Scholastic Press book from Scholastic Australia

This is the story of a young boy called Edward.

Edward was no ordinary child. He had a very special ability. Something **amazing** and unique and surprising . . . even to Edward!

Would you like to find out about it? **Let's go** . . .

C

Edward was a kind, friendly and eager-to-learn young boy, no doubt.

Edward was on the autism spectrum, and he could be quite shy. Especially around lots of kids at school.

Edward lived a wonderful, happy life at home with his family, who loved him very much—more than ***anything in the world.***

Edward had an older sister, Sarah. She didn't show an interest in most things, but Edward knew she loved her little brother (even if she didn't like to show it too much).

SAVE THE TURTLES
ANIMAL ENCOUNTERS-AUSTRALIA ZOO
DINOSAUR MUSEUM
Melbourne
ZOO
GENERAL ENTRY
2 x adult tickets
2 x childrens tickets
$ 60.30
edward
PERTH ZOO
SHOPPING LIST
Milk
Eggs
Bread for Sarah
Tea for Mum
Choccie

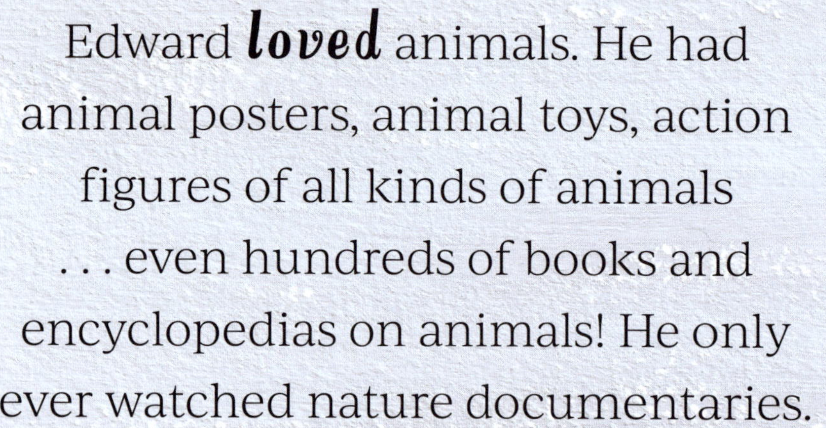

Edward ***loved*** animals. He had animal posters, animal toys, action figures of all kinds of animals . . . even hundreds of books and encyclopedias on animals! He only ever watched nature documentaries.

Edward loved animals so much, he often wished to be like them!

Little did he know that his wish would come true . . .

OCEAN FRIENDS

One fine day, Edward was sitting in the schoolyard with his best friend, Briana. Nearby, some other kids were playing in a loud and rowdy manner. This seemed normal to Briana, but to Edward it was too much.

Under his breath, Edward made a wish. 'I wish I was a tortoise, then I could hide from all this.'

As if on cue, **his wish came true!** In the blink of an eye, Edward went from being a human boy to a **Galapagos GIANT tortoise!**

Briana was scared at first, but then she saw Edward's kind eyes were still the same.

'It's okay, Eddie. Everything's calm now. You can come out of your shell,' she said.

Edward had found out he had a special ability. **He could turn into animals!** He was curious about it and wanted to show everyone, but his shyness got in the way.

However, Edward knew that he should tell his family, so later that night at home . . . Edward turned into a **bloodhound!**

'Mum, Dad, please calm down! It's me Edward!' he explained calmly. 'I wished I was a bloodhound and, well, here we are!'

'I can't believe this!' said his mother.

'This is lame,' said Sarah, unimpressed.

'How are you feeling?' asked his father.

'I still feel like myself,' said Edward.
'Except my tail is wagging, and I want
to scratch myself and chase a ball!'

'Well, it's a lot to take in but we still love you,
Edward. **No matter who or what you are**.'

ANIMALS
A–Z

The next day, Edward decided to be brave and tell his teacher, Miss Butler, all about his special ability. Miss Butler was the **kindest** teacher any child could want.

'Miss Butler, I have something to tell you,' he began. 'I don't know how or why this has happened . . .' Edward wasn't sure how to explain.

But before he could say anything else, there was a sudden cry for help!

'**Oh no!** Ben is stuck in the tree again,' Miss Butler said in dismay.

Edward then realised something. 'Miss Butler, I can show you instead!'

WEST ALCOTT
PUBLIC SCHOOL
BUGS
A
B
C
ANIMALS
A-Z

Edward went outside to the playground and took a deep breath. Then he said, 'I wish I was a **reticulated giraffe!**'

As his long, long neck stretched up as high as the tree, Edward moved closer to Ben. 'Hey, Ben. I'm here to help you get down. Do you trust me?'

Ben nervously replied, 'Yeah, I think I do.'

'Oh good,' Edward said. 'Because I don't want to be a **pain in the neck!** Get it?'

Ben chuckled timidly and then grabbed hold of Edward's tall neck. 'Thank you, Edward, you're the best giraffe ever! Would you like to be friends?'

Edward gently helped Ben to the ground, safe again. He smiled at his new friend. 'I'd love that.'

WEST ALCOTT
PUBLIC SCHOO

Miss Butler had been watching this from her classroom window with Briana, and was impressed by Edward's sudden courage!

'Edward, look what you can do when you believe in yourself!' Miss Butler beamed.

Edward was flattered and proud of himself. From that moment on, he made a decision: to **believe in himself**, stand up for others and help his fellow classmates whenever he could.

Later, Edward spotted another student named Mirjana being teased. She often got lost in a daydream during class and the other kids made fun of her for it. Edward wasn't going to let that carry on a second longer.

'I wish I was a **grizzly bear!**'

Edward roared at the bullies,
'Hey, leave her alone!'

The bullies ran away in fear.

'Thank you, Edward,' said Mirjana.
'I saw how you helped Ben the other day.
I'd love to be your friend too!'

Edward said, 'Consider it done, my new friend!'

Soon all the other kids began to hear about what Edward could do.

When two cheeky brothers named Jake and Callum were playing on the oval and got completely covered in mud, they called to Edward, 'Can you help us please?'

Edward thought for a moment and said, 'I know exactly what needs to be done! I wish I was an **African Elephant!**'

In a flash, Edward sprayed water over the two brothers and they were clean again! He then dried them off with his trunk.

'Thank you, Edward!' said Jake. 'You're a great pal!'

'You're **elephantastic**, Edward!' smiled Callum.

After many weeks of helping the kids at school, making new friends and assisting the teachers, Edward's confidence grew and grew.
His shyness faded away.

Edward helped Miss Butler in the classroom . . .

and played with all the kids at lunchtime . . .

and his **favourite thing of all** was helping the canteen staff clean up every day!

Let's learn about...
ANIMALS
CANTEEN

Edward had never been happier at school.

ANIMALS
A-Z

Edward learned that sometimes you have to be brave, and even if you feel unsure, it is always better to ***just be yourself***.

'You don't have to be like anyone else,' said his mother.

'Embrace who you are,' agreed his father.

Edward finally discovered that being yourself wasn't quite what he expected . . .

...it's even better.

ZOO TRIP 2025
ZOO TRIP 2025
ZOO TRIP 2025
ANIMAL A-Z

THE END

Every character in this book is named after some of my dearest friends in the world! These dedications are to show how much you mean the world to me, you have stood by me through the good and bad times and I am eternally grateful to you all, thank you for the wonderful friendships we share, I love you all very much!

My dearest friends; Hannah and Lawrence Murphy, Sarah Maxwell, Lincoln Jones, Jessica Tattersall, Ben Miller, Esme Louise James, Holly Fowler, Briana McKeogh, Mirjana Gligorevic and Dr Vanessa Pirotta.

In memory of Daws Butler, Phil Hartman and Don Messick, three of my heroes. Thank you for your inspiration—you are legends!

In memory of Jake and Callum Robinson. This is for you, Debra and Martin Robinson.

M.T.

To my younger self, who spent every waking moment drawing in quiet corners and dreaming of this wonderful life we've built.

E.B.